1. SSSSSnakes!
2. Rattle Trap
3. Click
4. Clank
5. Stair Scare
6. Step On It!
7. Tube Test
8. Who Nose?
9. Haze Maze
10. Crooked Creek
11. Ooze Views
12. Horror Hallways
13. What a Croc
14. Beat the Croc
15. Think Stink
16. Hold It
17. Hose Flows
18. Dig In
19. Running Nose
20. Charge It!
21. Pipe Down
22. Slow Drip

HORROR HALL

No Salesmen

WARNING...

You are about to enter Horror Hall, a frightening fortress filled with some of the most fiendishly flummoxing mazes known to creep or creature.

The only requirement for entry into Horror Hall is that you need to be a monster. This includes ogres, fiends, globs, ghouls, goons, spooks, giants, zombies, mummies, vampires, goblins, or any other sort of foul-smelling beast with hair on its body.

I'm glad you will be able to join us. My name is Schlocky Yuck, and the only thing I request before we begin is that you please keep the following Horror Hall rules in mind:
1. Refrain from being eaten by our monsters.
2. No flash photography.
3. All slime pits are for use by the staff only.
4. No peeking at the answers in the back of the book before you've really, really tried.
5. No mutating.

SSSSSNAKES!

Sssso nice to have you with us. At least one of these snakes thinks so. Can you figure out which snake's head leads to the tail that says "hi"?

HALL HUNT

Now that you're in Horror Hall, I feel it is only fair to tell you—there's no way out! Well, there is one secret escape hatch, but you'll have to solve a fiendish maze to find it. To make the maze even tougher, it has been torn in pieces and scattered throughout the book. The first piece is here. Solve it and you'll find out where to go next. Good luck. You'll need it!

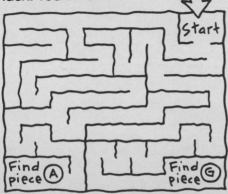

A B C D E F

RATTLE TRAP

I hope you appreciate the trouble our snake wrangler, Ed, has gone to to make your visit to Horror Hall as pleasant as possible. I'd especially like to point out his latest exhibit, a crate of highly venomous Transylvanian rattlers.

Oops! Oh, my, now Ed's gone and done it, hasn't he? He's knocked over the whole crate of rattlers. Perhaps you'd better be moving on. But can you?

Ed assures me there is a way through this slithering sea of vipers. For your own good I suggest you try to find it.

MONSTER MAZES

written, illustrated, and designed by
Patrick Merrell

Troll

Dedicated to

Printed in the United States of America.   ISBN 0-8167-4400-9

10 9 8 7 6 5 4 3 2 1

CLICK

Below are five ropes that have been locked together. If you wanted to separate them from each other, how many of the locks would you have to unlock? What if I said you could do it by unlocking only one of them? It's true! Can you figure out which one?

HALL A HUNT

Start!

Go to J

Go to G

CLANK

What a mess! These monsters that hang around Horror Hall are the biggest bunch of slobs I've ever seen.

Take these chains, for example. Please, take them. Well, not really, but at least take a look at them. As you do, you will notice that they are not only a mess—they are a maze! Starting at the chain link next to the big red arrow with the word "Start" on it, can you find your way to the lock at the end?

POOF

5 STAIR SCARE

There are several ways to get from "Start" to "End" in the maze of stairs below. But what if you could only go *up* seven stairs? You can go down as many stairs as you like, but you can't go up any more than seven stairs. Can you find the way through?

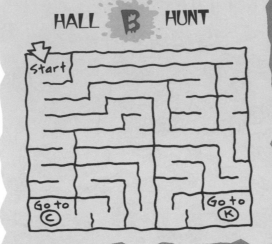

HALL B HUNT

Start

Go to C   Go to K

6 STEP ON IT!

This is one of my favorite spots in all of Horror Hall—the dungeon. Just look at all the wonderful mold. The cobwebs. The bones. Ahhh, it makes me feel right at home. But enough about me. My bet is that you'd like to find a way out of here as quickly as possible. Hah! You couldn't get out of here as quickly as possible if your life depended on it. Come to think of it, that may just be the case.

Beginning at the bottom, where Kirby is hanging out in his pit, can you find the one path that will get you up to the door?

End

Start

TUBE TEST

Welcome to the Horror Hall Lab. The experiment below is a tangle of beakers, test tubes, pipes, and hoses. Traveling through the red rubber hoses, can you find the route a drop of toad sweat would take to get from the medicine dropper to the large beaker at the bottom?

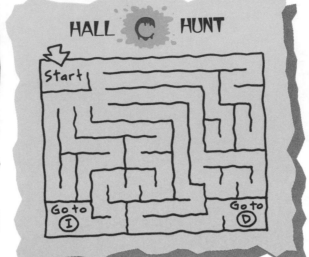

HALL **C** HUNT

Start

Go to
I

Go to
D

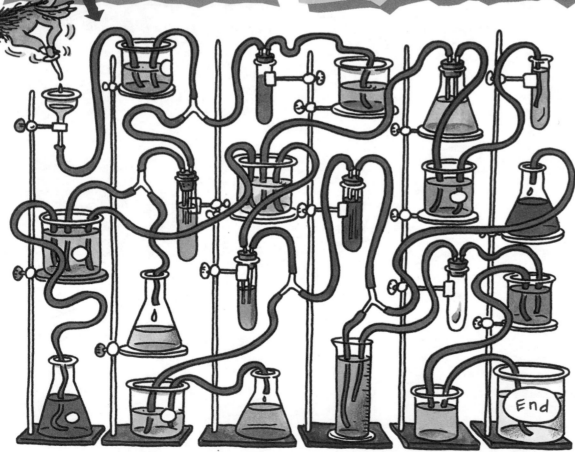

End

WHO NOSE?

Yeegads! It appears that Rumfeld, our resident mad scientist, has made a slight miscalculation in his latest experiment. Instead of mixing two dashes of zombie dust with one dram of toadstool powder, he's mixed fourteen gills of mummy paste with seven pecks of snake root. Or was it thirteen bushels of bat wings with nine gasps of hog's breath? Who knows—or should I say nose, because the sad truth is that Rumfeld has managed to change himself into a giant nose! Boy, has he blown it. Now everyone's going to be picking on him.

Luckily, he does have a batch of antidote to change himself back. The only question is, which faucet will give him a beaker full of antidote? *Starting at the lettered buckets,* can you figure it out for him?

Before   After

HAZE MAZE

Just look at that view—breath-gagging, isn't it! As nice as it is for us, though, our bats have a little trouble getting through it. Perhaps you could help them. Starting at the belfry, can you find a way through this maze of haze to the open sky in the upper right?

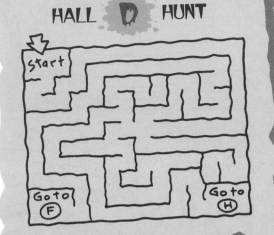

Start

Go to
F

Go to
H

CROOKED CREEK

There used to be twenty-four bridges crossing the creek in the backyard of Horror Hall. Unfortunately, a rare timber-eating ogre stopped by last week and made a stake sandwich out of them.

Melville, our groundskeeper, has managed to cut up a new pile of planks, but only enough to rebuild four of the bridges.

If Melville wanted to get from Crooked Cliff to Vulture Peak, which four spots should he choose to rebuild the bridges? (The dashed lines show the spots where the bridges can be placed.)

And hey, no swimming allowed!

End

Start

OOZE VIEWS

Have you ever wondered how a giant glob monster gets so big? The answer is actually very simple—lots of food goes in, but nothing ever comes out!

We decided to take a look inside our pal Globula to find out how this works. As you will see on the page to the left, the route through Globula's digestive system is a very complicated one. Lots of stomachs and gizzards and stuff.

Starting at Globula's mouth, can you find the route that a meal takes to get to Globula's storage cavity?

HALL HUNT

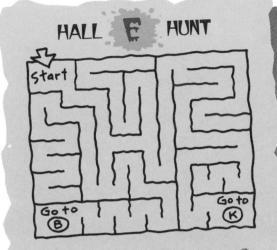

HORROR HALLWAYS

Well, I must admit I'm glad to see you're still alive and kicking. I'd hate to think you weren't able to make it far enough to be tripped up by this next brain-tangling torture test I have planned for you.

As you'll soon see, this maze is actually two mazes in one. That's because it takes place on two floors of Horror Hall. The object is to get from the red Skeleton's Closet on the third floor to the green Lizard's Lounge on the second floor. Sounds simple enough, doesn't it? Well, nothing is simple in Horror Hall.

Along the way, you'll have to try and avoid plenty of dead ends, wrong turns, and worse. I just love the worse parts. Also, keep in mind that you'll probably have to go back and forth between the two floors more than once to get through. Can you do it?

2ⁿᵈ FLOOR

End

Lizard's Lounge

Bottomless Pit

Mummy's Tomb

A B C D E F G H

WHAT A CROC

Our favorite television show, *Beat the Croc*, is just about to come on. Unfortunately, one of these four crocs has swallowed the end of the TV's electrical cord. Starting at the crocs, can you figure out which croc's mouth we should pry open so that we can plug in the TV?

HALL F HUNT

Start

Go to B

Go to H

BEAT THE CROC

"Greetings ghouls, goblins, and goons. It's time once again for everygrubby's favorite ghastly game show . . . Beat the Croc. Tonight, our contestants are Seymour, a near-sighted cyclops from Long Eyeland, and I.W., a giant from East Rutherford, New Jersey. For tonight's show we're going to pit Seymour and I.W. against the Croc in a dash across the pit of doom. Our contestants will have four minutes to get from start to finish. Once again, should either of them fail to make it in time, they'll be getting to know our Croc a little better...."

Are you up to the challenge? All you have to do is find a path from the contestants' starting spot to the finish line. You have four minutes.

1
2
3
4

BEAT THE CROC

THINK STINK

Below is a haunted stinkplant. Because the smell from a haunted stinkplant only goes up, it's always a good idea to put it in a high place. If I wanted to put the haunted stinkplant on top of this pile of bricks, what spot should I choose so that it would be in the highest place?

HOLD IT

This probably looks like your run-of-the-mill haunted stinkplant, doesn't it? Correct. And because you're correct, you have won the honor of trying to find a way through this haunted stinkplant's incredibly tangled roots.

Just one problem—the smell. A haunted stinkplant smells bad. How bad? Imagine 17 ogres in a garbage dump eating Gorgonzola cheese. That's the smell of a stinkplant—on a good day.

So here's a suggestion—hold your breath. That's right. Get ready, take a deep breath, and then start solving. If you can't make it all the way, stop, take another breath, and then continue on from there. How many breaths will you need? I've made up a chart for you to see how you rate:

1 breath: Iron Lung
2 breaths: Oxygen Tank
3 breaths: Gasbag
4 or more: Leaky Balloon

HOSE FLOWS

Out in the backyard we've arranged a quick hose test for you. The hoses in the two pictures below may look the same, but they are not. In which of these two pictures will the water flow through the hose so that it fills up the hole on the other side?

HALL H HUNT

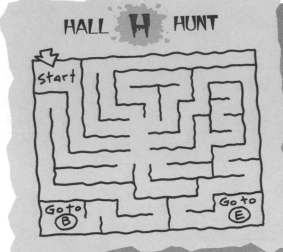

Start

Go to B

Go to E

DIG IN

Ratty Patty, one of our favorite ghouls here at Horror Hall, has been digging for lost relatives in the backyard. So far, no luck, but the effort hasn't been a total waste. As it turns out, the holes—some of which are connected by tunnels—make up a very interesting maze.

To help you out, Patty has put a sign with a drawing on it next to each hole. Holes marked with the same drawing are connected by a tunnel. If you follow the signs and paths in just the right way, there is a route from the old tree stump to the swamp.

Can you figure it out?

A

B

19. RUNNING NOSE

Holy honkers! Not only has Rumfeld's anti-nose serum worn off, but he's left the rest of it uncovered. In order to save it, he has to cover it up in *28 seconds or less.* Figuring that it takes him one second to run across each square, can you find a way for him to do it?

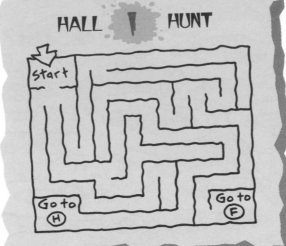

HALL HUNT

Start

Go to H

Go to F

20. CHARGE IT!

Uh-oh. Rumfeld is attempting another one of his experiments. This time he appears to be following in the tragic footsteps of Dr. Frankenstein by trying to reanimate a once-living creature through the use of a high voltage electrical jolt.

There is one slight difference, though. Rumfeld's creature is a giant celery stalk. What the purpose of this experiment might be is something only Rumfeld could tell us. Unfortunately, with Rumfeld in his present form, I don't think we're going to be able to understand anything he says. Then again, maybe that's a good thing.

In any event, your challenge in this misguided attempt at science is to try to find a route from the cloud in the upper right, through the lightning bolt, and down to the table holding Rumfeld's giant celery stalk. Go ahead, give it a crack!

A giant celery has been stalking the neighborhood...

PIPE DOWN

There is an old section of pipe that needs to be replaced in the basement. Below, you will see seven sections of new pipe that have been made to replace it. Only one of them is put together in exactly the same shape. Can you figure out which section it is?

HALL J HUNT

Start

Go to C

Go to I

SLOW DRIP

Zoe, our zombie plumber, may not be the fastest, and she may not be the brightest, but she sure is thorough. Two and a half years ago, when we had a leak in one of the pipes down in the cellar, Zoe shuffled right down there. Yesterday, when she finished, not only was the leak gone, but we found ourselves with a fine maze to boot.

You will see her handiwork on the next page. Beginning at the water tank, can you find the route the water takes through this jumble of pipes to get to the faucet at the end?

OLD SECTION

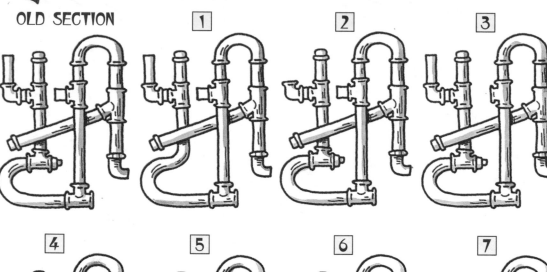

1

2

3

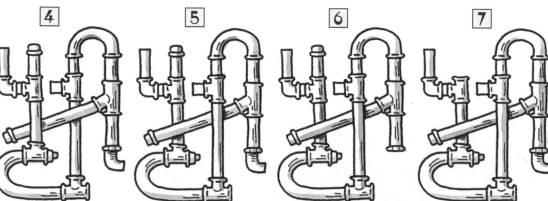

4

5

6

7

HALL  HUNT

Congratulations. Not many people make it this far in our Hall Hunt. But before you go patting yourself on the back, let me remind you that you still have one last piece of maze to get through—and it may not be as easy as you think.

Sure, getting to the secret escape hatch is simple, but that's not going to do you much good without a key to open it. What you need to do first is find a route that takes you to the key. Once you have the key, then you need to find a path to the secret escape hatch.

Do all that, and then you can pat yourself on the back. Fail, and I'm afraid you'll have one of Rumfeld's creations patting you on the back. . . .

ANSWERS

1 SSSSSNAKES!: C

3 CLICK: 3

5 STAIR SCARE

2 RATTLE TRAP

4 CLANK

6 STEP ON IT!

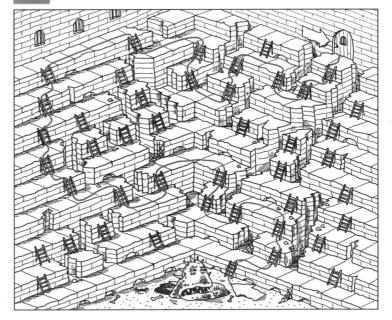

7 TUBE TEST

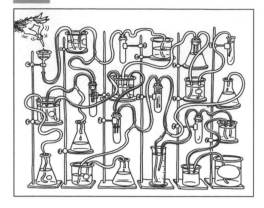

8 WHO NOSE?: E

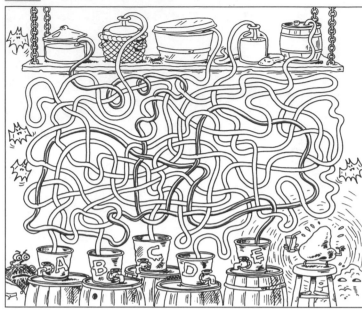

9 HAZE MAZE

10 CROOKED CREEK

11 OOZE VIEWS

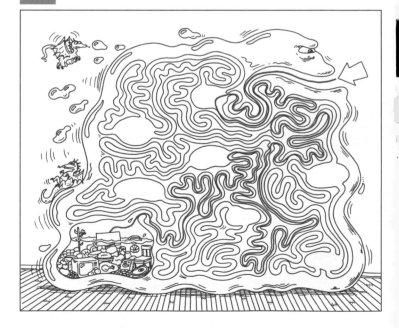

12 HORROR HALLWAYS

13
WHAT A CROC: 2

14 BEAT THE CROC

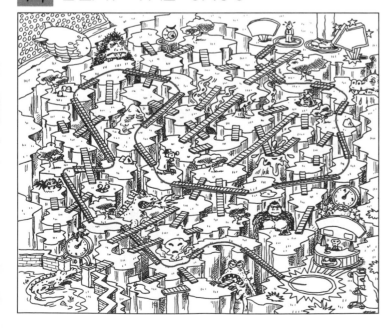

15
THINK STINK: C

17
HOSE FLOWS: B

16 HOLD IT

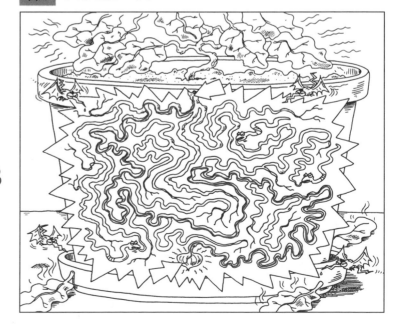

18 DIG IN

19 RUNNING NOSE

K HALL HUNT

20 CHARGE IT!

21

PIPE
DOWN: 5

22 SLOW DRIP